Purr and Get Rich!

Create the Mischief you Want to See in the World

BOOK *Mayhem*™

MOGUL DIVISION

WWW.MOGULDIVISION.COM

From the Desk of Harry K. Juniper
Chief of Mischief at Book Mayhem

Greetings,

I can't help but notice that one of two things transpired here:

1) Either you're a very twisted person that likes messing with people's minds,

or

2) You have amazing friends that gifted you this little gem.

Regardless, thank you for getting this book (and I use the term book loosely).

You are about to embark on a journey where you will need to master your poker face. I know that hiding your smirk will become very difficult in the presence of the ingenious publication you are currently holding.

As you have obviously discovered, this is not a book. It is, instead, a notebook designed to play with the minds of people who fail to mind their own business. Just between you and me – that's most people.

The cover and format of this notebook has been specially designed to look like a real book. Our book covers are either completely silly or just on this side of offensive without crossing over. (Although I'm sure someone has been offended by now.)

Think of this book as the ultimate prank tool for introverts. It is a silent way of turning heads. If you ever have a bad day, you can be certain that you will feel a bit better after you have started people whispering. It's the gift that keeps on giving.

Don't worry. You can actually use this as a functional notebook if you so desire. Alternatively, you can simply leave it on your coffee table, office, washroom, or bookcase and kick-start some interesting conversations.

As per our lawyers, I can't guarantee anything. But deep in my heart I know that you will become the life of the party, the enabler of laughs, the magician who turns frowns upside down with this simple book.

Have fun, don't get in too much trouble, and buy more of our "books!"

(They make perfect gifts, for the people you love, and even the people you hate.)

Sincerely,
Harry K. Juniper,
Chief of Mischief at Book Mayhem

Create the Mischief you Want to See in the World

BOOK Mayhem

Create the Mischief you Want to See in the World

Create the Mischief you Want to See in the World

BOOK Mayhem

Create the Mischief you Want to See in the World

Create the Mischief you Want to See in the World

Create the Mischief you Want to See in the World

BOOK *Mayhem*

Create the Mischief you Want to See in the World

BOOK *Mayhem*

Create the Mischief you Want to See in the World

Create the Mischief you Want to See in the World

Create the Mischief you Want to See in the World

Create the Mischief you Want to See in the World

BOOK Mayhem

Create the Mischief you Want to See in the World

Create the Mischief you Want to See in the World

BOOK *Mayhem*

Create the Mischief you Want to See in the World

BOOK Mayhem

Create the Mischief you Want to See in the World

BOOK Mayhem

Create the Mischief you Want to See in the World

Create the Mischief you Want to See in the World

Create the Mischief you Want to See in the World

BOOK Mayhem

Create the Mischief you Want to See in the World

Create the Mischief you Want to See in the World

Create the Mischief you Want to See in the World

BOOK Mayhem

Create the Mischief you Want to See in the World

BOOK Mayhem

Create the Mischief you Want to See in the World

BOOK Mayhem

Create the Mischief you Want to See in the World

Create the Mischief you Want to See in the World

BOOK Mayhem

Create the Mischief you Want to See in the World

Create the Mischief you Want to See in the World

BOOK *Mayhem*

Create the Mischief you Want to See in the World

BOOK *Mayhem*

Create the Mischief you Want to See in the World

Create the Mischief you Want to See in the World

Create the Mischief you Want to See in the World

Create the Mischief you Want to See in the World

BOOK Mayhem

Create the Mischief you Want to See in the World

BOOK Mayhem

Create the Mischief you Want to See in the World

BOOK Mayhem

Create the Mischief you Want to See in the World

Create the Mischief you Want to See in the World

Create the Mischief you Want to See in the World

Create the Mischief you Want to See in the World

BOOK *Mayhem*

Create the Mischief you Want to See in the World

Create the Mischief you Want to See in the World

Create the Mischief you Want to See in the World

BOOK Mayhem

Create the Mischief you Want to See in the World

BOOK Mayhem

Create the Mischief you Want to See in the World

Create the Mischief you Want to See in the World

BOOK *Mayhem*

Create the Mischief you Want to See in the World

BOOK Mayhem

Create the Mischief you Want to See in the World

Create the Mischief you Want to See in the World

Create the Mischief you Want to See in the World

Create the Mischief you Want to See in the World

Create the Mischief you Want to See in the World

Create the Mischief you Want to See in the World

BOOK Mayhem

Create the Mischief you Want to See in the World

Create the Mischief you Want to See in the World

Create the Mischief you Want to See in the World

BOOK *Mayhem*

Create the Mischief you Want to See in the World

Create the Mischief you Want to See in the World

Create the Mischief you Want to See in the World

BOOK *Mayhem*

Create the Mischief you Want to See in the World

BOOK Mayhem

Create the Mischief you Want to See in the World

BOOK Mayhem

Create the Mischief you Want to See in the World

Create the Mischief you Want to See in the World

BOOK Mayhem

Create the Mischief you Want to See in the World

BOOK Mayhem

Create the Mischief you Want to See in the World

BOOK Mayhem

Create the Mischief you Want to See in the World

Create the Mischief you Want to See in the World

BOOK Mayhem

Create the Mischief you Want to See in the World

BOOK Mayhem

Create the Mischief you Want to See in the World

BOOK *Mayhem*

Create the Mischief you Want to See in the World

Create the Mischief you Want to See in the World

BOOK Mayhem

Create the Mischief you Want to See in the World

Create the Mischief you Want to See in the World

Create the Mischief you Want to See in the World

BOOK Mayhem

Create the Mischief you Want to See in the World

BOOK *Mayhem*

Create the Mischief you Want to See in the World

BOOK Mayhem

Create the Mischief you Want to See in the World

Create the Mischief you Want to See in the World

BOOK *Mayhem*

Create the Mischief you Want to See in the World

BOOK Mayhem

Create the Mischief you Want to See in the World

BOOK Mayhem

Create the Mischief you Want to See in the World

BOOK *Mayhem*

Create the Mischief you Want to See in the World

BOOK *Mayhem*

Create the Mischief you Want to See in the World

Create the Mischief you Want to See in the World

BOOK Mayhem

Create the Mischief you Want to See in the World

Create the Mischief you Want to See in the World

BOOK Mayhem

Create the Mischief you Want to See in the World

Create the Mischief you Want to See in the World

BOOK Mayhem

Create the Mischief you Want to See in the World

BOOK *Mayhem*

Create the Mischief you Want to See in the World

BOOK Mayhem

Create the Mischief you Want to See in the World

Create the Mischief you Want to See in the World

Create the Mischief you Want to See in the World

BOOK Mayhem

Create the Mischief you Want to See in the World

BOOK Mayhem

Collect all our Notebooks!

27070690R00119

Made in the USA
San Bernardino, CA
08 December 2015